# The Discrimination-Free Celebrant

*Unravelling our Prejudices and Biases*

By Veronika Sophia Robinson

Published by Celebrant Collection,
An imprint of Starflower Press

Cover illustration by Sarah Esau

*The Discrimination-Free Celebrant*
© Veronika Sophia Robinson
© Cover illustration by Sarah Esau
Published by Celebrant Collection,
an imprint of Starflower Press
Full Moon in Virgo, February 2024
978-1-7385324-2-1

This book has been written for Heart-led Celebrants and our celebrants-in-training. It is, however, available to other celebrants. The language, style and teaching is reflective of how we train new celebrants and our non-dualistic beliefs about humanity. It's neither a tome nor treatise, but a gentle wake-up call to unite us in compassion for our fellow humans. It isn't designed to turn you (or me!) into a saint or make you squeaky clean and free of your own opinions. It's an invitation to go within. The intention is to make us aware. It is humbly offered as a guide towards Best-Practice Celebrancy.

# Discrimination-free Celebrancy Statement

I practise discrimination-free celebrancy.

This means that I will not discriminate (or associate with those who discriminate) against you on the grounds of religion or other beliefs, disability, mental health, race, culture, gender, gender reassignment, age, body shape or size or adornment, health narrative, financial, marital or parental status.

I honour the right of each human being to celebrate their life.

You have my assurance that I will accord you the respect you deserve.

## Heart-led Celebrant Affirmation

May I serve with integrity.
Show me how to live with a loving heart,
and accept all human beings
as I would wish to be accepted.

May I open up to the vast possibilities
of my creative self,
and share these with grace, humility and flair.

I offer myself as a channel of peace, harmony,
joy, beauty and balance.

In my visible and invisible work,
may I make this world a more beautiful place.

May I go gently into this day.

## Dedication

I wrote this book for myself,
and I wrote it for you.

But most importantly,
I wrote it for them: those who've been
maligned, bullied, tortured, tormented,
teased, and ridiculed.

One day we'll all wake up.

*When you understand every opinion
is a vision loaded with history,
you will start to understand that
all judgement is a confession.*
- Nicola Tesla

# Chapters

"What if our religion was each other.
If our practice was our life.
If prayer, our words.
What if the temple was the Earth.
If forests were our church.
If holy water - the rivers, lakes, and ocean.
What if meditation was our relationships.
If the teacher was life.
If wisdom was self-knowledge.
If love was the centre of our being."
~ Ganga White

Before you read any further, take some time to write down what you, at this moment, believe discrimination to be. No cheating, just write whatever naturally comes to mind.

"We don't see the world as it is,
we see it as we are."
- Anais Nin

# What is Discrimination?

As you read this book, and reflect on the different ways people look, express, think, believe, act and live their lives, also consider various words that can be included with, next-to, or under the word *discriminate*.

To discriminate is to *'recognise and identify someone as separate and distinct'*.

It may show up in the way we:
- judge
- criticise
- favour
- select
- individualise
- hate
- separate
- victimise
- show bias
- set apart
- incline
- choose
- treat differently
- cultivate
- treat as inferior
- have opinions

As a result, we may be prudent, pernickety, picky, finical. Our lack of respect for other people's cultures, ways of being and beliefs can lead to discrimination, exploitation and the denial of people's rights.

**This book will ask you to look at the ways you judge others.**

*Why do you carry those judgements?*
*Who taught you them?*
*Can you state them to be categorically true?*
*Can you tell the difference between a preconceived idea and the truth?*

# In Each Other's Shoes

Writing this book has caused me to dig deep and acknowledge my biases, and also to articulate when I have been discriminated against and the impact it has had on my life.

Yes, I come from the vantage of white privilege, and there are certain things I'll never have the experience of or fully understand how it shapes one's life.

I do know what it's like to be on the receiving end of judgement, cruelty, criticism, bias and discrimination.

Don't diminish your experience because it wasn't as big or obvious as someone else's experience.

I don't have brown or black skin, attend a church, mosque, temple, nor am I gay. Therefore, I'm unable to speak of those experiences from the point of view of being discriminated against. I can, however, speak from the truth of being a discrimination-free celebrant who openly welcomes others. For example, the first wedding ceremony I ever officiated was for two women. The year was 1995, long before celebrants added rainbows to their websites. Heck, I didn't even have a website back then.

I am accepting, have compassion and empathy, and an ability to step outside of my own skin and thinking. I have the awareness, and in some cases, the experience of what it is like to be segregated, ousted, hated, misunderstood, vilified, judged, attacked or ignored.

In one way or another, I've tended to live at the fringes. This has been the story of my life. I chose to become vegetarian when I was just five years of age. A year or so later, we moved to a rural property of 700 acres where my father decided to raise beef cattle. In fact, all around us were farmers. They'd all say to me "You'll die. You have to have protein!" More than half a century later, and there's no sign of any protein deficiency. It might be hard to imagine it, given how common it is now for people to adopt a vegetarian diet; but, back then, it was like being an alien. Growing up in beef-cattle country taught me what it's like to be *different*. Not just that, but it was a predominately Catholic area and I, well, my leanings were towards spirituality. And, as if

I didn't have enough of the fringe factor, I was the daughter of German immigrants in rural Australia.

When I became a mother and home educated our children, there were always loads of judgements sent my way.

For these reasons, and plenty more, I offer this book to implore *all* celebrants, whether they have trained and certified with us as Heart-led Celebrants, or trained elsewhere, to be living, shining examples of acceptance, always working from a place of kindness, integrity and compassion. We don't have to agree or understand someone's lifestyle to be open and accepting. It costs nothing to be kind and treat people with the same respect we'd like. The only thing that stops us doing so is ignorance and/or arrogance.

While I know the majority of people do not like books with questions, this *has* been designed as a workbook. I make no apologies for that. To understand what it means to be discrimination-free, we have to *bring up anything unlike it for healing; and to explore and study it so we can create a celebrant practice of inclusivity and acceptance.*

The seed for this book had to settle within me for a few years. I'd been on the committee of a celebrant organisation, and left due to discrimination by one of the leading figures towards various members of the association. It rattled me for a long time that someone who was working as a celebrant, and in a position of leadership amongst celebrants, would be homophobic, misogynistic, racist, and blatantly body shame our celebrant members when so many of us in the celebrant world are actively trying to promote and live a path of inclusivity.

I was at a loss how to deal with this as that person, and those around them on the committee, were unwilling to acknowledge the discrimination. Their willingness to entertain such behaviour was incongruous. Perhaps they were tone deaf to such things? Despite speaking up, *several* times, my words fell on deaf ears. I also came to respect my own integrity and recognise that it's not enough to 'not discriminate' but I also had to distance myself from those who do. And so, I resigned from my role as President on the committee and continued with my own celebrant journey. My inclusivity statement also includes that 'I will not associate with those who discriminate'. I left that association with a deep sense of frustration and sought to ensure that anyone and everyone who trained with us at Heart-led Ceremonies Celebrant Training truly understood what it means to be a discrimination-free celebrant. It has also meant that we've turned people away from our training when it's been clear (in their own words) that they have 'no intention of working with certain types of people'.

From time to time, I have posted on my social media the following statement:

> This means that I will not discriminate (*or associate with those who discriminate*) against you on the grounds of religion or other beliefs, disability, mental health, race, culture, gender, gender reassignment, sexuality, age, body shape or size or adornment, health narrative, financial, marital or parental status. I honour the right of each human being to celebrate their life.

It's interesting to me that some celebrants comment  rather angrily in response with phrases such as: "No celebrants discriminate!"

My experience, not just with the aforementioned association, but as witnessed first-hand in conversations at celebrant conferences, networking, workshops and by observation on social media and forums has been otherwise, and that remains so. The purpose of this book is not to name or shame, but to shine a light for each of us to look more closely at our held beliefs. Oftentimes, people aren't even aware of just how they're discriminating.

Where do our prejudices and biases come from? Are they inherently ours or shaped by the influence of parents, teachers, friends, peers and colleagues, religion, culture, media?

This book aims to unravel what it is that has caused humans, for too many years to count, to destroy, belittle, annihilate another because they are *different*. At the end of these pages, it is hoped that you will feel confident in practising discrimination-free celebrancy, and that you will feel strong and articulate enough to speak up about *any* and *all* acts of discrimination (personally and professionally). This has been designed to challenge, educate, inspire and motivate you towards a celebrant practice based on integrity, awareness and acceptance.

My own journey to reach this point has been driven by an innate awareness that, in the words of Ram Dass, *'we are all just walking each other Home'*. I believe that, although we live in different bodies, and each has our own life's journey to undertake, we are all connected by an invisible thread. This same cord stitches together *every* living being upon this planet.

In my own life, I've had many opportunities to learn about others who were different to me, and to find our connection. It started quite early in my life with our neighbours who were Jehovah's Witnesses. As someone who was raised absolutely loving Christmas, it was a new experience for me to meet people who didn't celebrate the festive season or their birthdays. This was one of my first experiences of 'reframing'.

Raised in rural Australia, my experience of aboriginal people was seeing them drunk in the gutters of our local town. It would have been so easy to make judgements and see them as 'less than' if I'd listened to the cultural narrative. Aboriginals aren't born alcoholics. Situations like this have come about because of white man's interference, and taking them far away from their natural life 'in the bush'.

A referendum ballot asked Australians to vote on a proposed law: *To alter the Constitution to recognise the First Peoples of Australia by establishing an Aboriginal and Torres Strait Islander Voice.* (One Voice) The year was 2023, and I cried for days at the absurdity that something like this even needs a vote, and that so many people voted against it. "In this day and age!" I kept repeating to myself.

During my school years, one of my classmates was called Karen. To this day, I can still see her thick, cropped, copper-red hair, and how she was at least a foot taller than me, and stockier. Her voice was deeper, too. I sensed that she never fitted in (I was never popular, bullied daily, so was sensitive to others who too were ousted in some way). It was only later in life that I learned Karen became Karl. I hope they've found peace far away from the bullies in the school playground. I can only begin to imagine the inner torment Karen experienced, back then in the mid eighties, when the world was less open to other ways of living and being. They say that school prepares us for life. Does it prepare us or is it a microcosm of the discrimination of children's parents?

Each day of my schooling involved a long bus journey on the rural route to school. A school bus can be its own version of hell: all those unruly kids crammed into a moving metal tin. There was one particular family on our route: the Harveys; they were dirt poor. It was obvious not just from the ramshackle wooden house they lived in, perched at the end of a narrow dusty track, but their ill-fitting raggedy clothes, unkempt hair and unwashed faces. Every part of their being stood out in bright neon lights. It still makes me nauseas, some 46 or so years later, how the children in that family were treated. They couldn't get on or off the bus without a whole lot of kids leaning out the windows and spitting on them. The bus driver NEVER stopped anyone from doing it. Can you imagine? As if childhood doesn't have enough drama. And school itself isn't necessarily a great place to have to spend the bulk of your formative years. But to be spat on, twice a day? Just because your parents didn't have a lot of income?

I remember on a celebrant forum someone asking how other celebrants would feel about doing the funeral of someone like Ian Brady (the Moors Murderer). It's fair to say it was pretty unanimous that celebrants wouldn't do it. Comments were along the lines of 'I wouldn't spit on his grave!' In our celebrant training, I ask our students to think about the question: "does everyone deserve a funeral?" After some thought, most of them say "Yes" because they recognise that no matter how evil that person may have been, they weren't born that way. Each of us began life as a precious, innocent baby. Officiating the funeral of someone that society has ousted, for reasons such as those above, doesn't mean we condone their behaviour.

Early in my working life, I taught at a Montessori school, one-to-one with a young boy, Sam, who had Down Syndrome. Oh dear Sam! The boy with the biggest smile, and best hugs ever, and not to mention his ability to somehow *always* end up on the school roof (we never did figure out how he did it!).

Sam's mother, who had four other children, never doubted that Sam would grow up into a fine young man, get a job, and enjoy his life. And nor did I. I did, however, have to deal with his snotty noses, and hard-to-decipher words, on a daily basis. But oh how I loved him! And he loved me. Till the day I die, Sam will always hold a dear place in my heart.

I once heard someone say that if she ever gave birth to a Down Syndrome baby she'd flush it down the toilet. Those words still make me ill to my core. They haunt me. The truth is that for all the education we have, there will always be people who are so mired in judgement, criticism and lack of connection. Perhaps we'll never have a world where we can 'live and let live' and celebrate each person's uniqueness. But I live in hope.

I've since had the opportunity and pleasure to meet and work with many people who have Down Syndrome, such as when I worked in a Rudolph Steiner Boarding School for teenagers with intellectual challenges. As a celebrant, I've had the honour of officiating their funerals, too, and speaking about the fullness of the lives they lived.

Could it be that right from the moment we arrive in this world, or earlier when our image is captured on a scan, that there are people all around ready to judge and pigeonhole us into some sort of category? When we're born, we are: weighed, measured, named, gender assigned, and so on. Did we meet our APGAR scores adequately? Within minutes and hours, people have made decisions about who we are.

But who are we really? *Really*? We are children of the universe, no less than the trees and the stars, and we have a right to be here (to quote Desiderata).

Blessed to be raised on a horse stud in rural Australia, I pretty well grew up on the back of a horse. Freedom to roam, gallop across fields, endurance ride for miles, or meander up invisible mountain trails, ensured I knew what being removed from limitations felt like. In my late teens, I volunteered for various charities, including Riding for Disabled. The joy I experienced watching others, who will have felt limited in so many ways by the body (and mind) they were born into, suddenly experience greater movement and vantage points was wonderful! Week after week, a whole new world opened up to them. And I like to think that people, like myself, allowed them to experience this because we were warm, welcoming, kind and opened the door.

And honestly, that is a large and vital part of living a discrimination-free life. To open the door, and say "Welcome, come inside" or "Hey, welcome to my world. Want to play? Or have an adventure?" or "Show me your world. What is life like for you?"

During the years before I became a mother, I also volunteered in a hospice, spending hours visiting patients and just listening or reading. It might seem that people wouldn't judge those who are dying, but you'd be surprised! It was here, at the bedsides of those slowly slipping away from this Earth, that I found my own inner healing.

Other ways I gave my time to those in the community included volunteering for Meals on Wheels: delivering cooked food to those who were housebound or no longer able to cook for themselves. I cherished those moments when I was the one invited across the threshold; and in whatever precious moments we shared together as I unwrapped their hot food and placed it before them, I listened and practised the art of presence-ing. If we're honest, insightful, and willing to truly explore what it means to accept another human being, it is about being present. I don't suppose I was conscious of what I was doing at the time. It was instinctive.

As celebrants, we often talk about 'holding the space', and yet I wonder if, for many celebrants, it only refers to the ceremony itself. To hold the space is something that applies to *all* aspects of our work, including the way we provide an open and loving container to all those who inhabit this world.

There are two phrases which guide me in life:
*To walk in another's shoes*
and
*There but for the grace of God go I.*

As an adult, I've attempted to be multilingual so that I stretch out of my English-only mindset. Learning my parents' native tongue of German has been a lot easier than learning Welsh, like my granddaughter.

As a woman of 'white privilege', I constantly seek to educate myself, and those around me. I also know what it is like to be discriminated (judged, criticised) against, and understand that it comes in many forms. As I share a few examples from my own life, it might bring to mind some of your own experiences.

My body shape is top heavy. It's certainly not something I'd have chosen for myself. Why people think they have the right to joke about a woman's breasts is beyond me. Throughout my life people have openly commented as if it's their right to body shame me.

I've always been someone whose way of thinking strayed from the mainstream. Words like 'weird', 'hippy' and 'unusual' have not always been given in kindness. I don't consider myself to be a hippy or weird. Unusual, for sure. I simply don't 'fit' into people's neatly designed categories.

Many times, my gender has been held against me. That, of course, has made me strive harder.

Being a truth teller has caused no end of problems in my life as people sought to 'shut me up'. When working as a reporter for a local newspaper, I uncovered some criminal activity by a local business. Despite my solid evidence, could I report it? Hell no! The newspaper relied on the company's advertising revenue.

For a time, I worked as a phlebotomist taking blood samples from people (don't ask how, I can't bear to see people in discomfort) in a hospital. My new boss started sexually harassing me. This had a huge impact on me and my health and I dreaded going into work. Eventually, I spoke to the general manager of the hospital. Was I supported? Was my boss in the laboratory reprimanded or held to account? The manager said to me that "it's easier for us to hire a new phlebotomist than to find a new scientist. Look for another job." After taking my complaint to the Ombudsman, there was an eventual law change to ensure sexual harassment was treated seriously in Queensland hospitals.

If there's anything I've learned from various experiences in my life, it is this: *we must speak up when there is unfairness, injustice, bullying and discrimination*. It can show its face in many different ways.

I remember when I was bullied and victimised by the Egg Industry Board. During my time as a media officer for the Royal New Zealand Society for the Prevention of Cruelty to Animals, I launched the Ban the Battery Cage campaign to bring an end to the cruel and abhorrent practice of keeping laying hens in cages (for their whole lives) the size of an A4 page.

As a defender of the underdog, or in that case, underchicken (who was defecated on by all the chickens in cages above), I was vocal, passionate and outspoken. However, what is important to remember is that at all times *I spoke the truth*. As an investigative journalist,

I dealt in facts. My articles in the media highlighted where our eggs came from, and the cruel journey from 'farm' to plate.

My boss at the time, a sweet but frail elderly man, called me into his office. There were six men from the Egg Industry Board who wanted me hauled in (and no doubt put into one of their damn hen cages!). I watched these men, all sitting there as if they ran the world, try and bully me into submission. They were clear about one thing: they had to stop me. I was having an impact on their lucrative industry. Even though I was in my early twenties, in that moment I'd never felt so powerful. My words had power. People were listening.

They tried various underhand tactics to silence me, eventually giving in when I wouldn't back down. In the end, the only thing they could do to convince me to stop publishing articles was to say that eggs were "cheap food and helpful for single mothers on a low income". It meant they'd be able to feed their kids. My response? "Lentils are an economical choice too!" As an aside, a few months ago (as I write this book in 2023) battery cages have now *finally* been phased out in New Zealand.

When people discriminate (and whatever variant word you use), it comes from ignorance or lack of understanding. After having my dead baby removed from my womb, by a surgical procedure known as Dilation and Evacuation, which happens after 24 weeks gestation, I could feel myself coming out of anaesthetic. Crying my broken heart out, my grief was overwhelming. I was utterly distraught. The doctor snapped at me: "What are you crying for? It was dead!" This example might not be one you'd associate with discrimination. After all, it's not to do with the usual qualifiers of skin colour or religion or socio-economic status.

**Unravel**
Thinking about the story above, write down why the doctor was discriminatory.

**Unravel**

Looking back across the years of your life, write down some of the different ways you've been judged, bullied, ostracised, victimised.

These are *your* experiences, and it doesn't matter how minor you (or others) might deem them to be. What is important is to shine a light on them so you can bring them out of the shadows and extend awareness to others who might experience something similar.

Discrimination is as rife in celebrancy as any other part of life, whether it is due to the colour of the celebrant's skin and being given less work; or clients warned their celebrant isn't white; or a celebrant not taking on clients who have different coloured skin to them; or celebrants using words like bridezilla or pauper's funeral; or not taking on 'fat' or 'ugly' brides, or wedding couples with disabilities because they want the photos on their website to look good. Don't believe it's true? Think again.

The intention of this book is that you will come away with a greater sense of

- Curiosity about others
- Welcoming tendency
- Care
- Kindness
- Acceptance
- Inclusivity
- Our oneness

These changes can happen overnight or maybe it'll be a gradual awakening as you start adapting to new ways of being, learning and loving.

# Prejudices & Biases

Whenever we make prejudicial or unfair distinctions between people, we are discriminating. This is regardless of whether it's about class, race, age, gender, sexuality, body shape, health narrative, finances and so on.

I was driving along one of our rural roads, admiring the sunlight and shadows as they slipped across the fellside and fields, when one of the songs from my Katie Melua CD came on. The lyrics stop me in my tracks every time I hear them.

> *If a black man is racist, is it okay?*
> *When it's the white man's racism*
> *that made him that way...*

**Unravel**
What are your thoughts on the question in those lyrics?

Explore how you feel when you read those words. Say them out loud.

Elsewhere in the song, I'm brought to a pause.

*Because the line between,*
*Wrong and right,*
*Is the width of a thread,*
*From a spider's web.*

Again, such powerful lyrics.

**Unravel**

At what point does a remark or observation about someone's difference/s become a bias or prejudice?

How slim is that threshold between right and wrong?

As we unravel the threads of our thinking, our judgements, our beliefs about people, we become more and more conscious of the width of that thread between right and wrong.

Katie kept singing, and I sang along with her:

*The piano keys are black and white,*
*But they sound like a million colours*
*in your mind.*

It's a strange thing, this being human. Many people crave community and connection, and desire to be with 'like-minded' people. There's comfort in being around those who are the same. But only to a certain degree. Imagine being with someone who looked exactly like you, spoke like you, dressed like you, had your mannerisms and so on. At what point does that sameness become unsettling? One moment we want sameness and the next we're craving our own identity. They say that imitation is the sincerest form of flattery. But it might well be the most annoying thing, too. What is it we're looking for? We seek connection, yes. We want to know that you and he/she/they and I are all okay.

It's a beautiful thing that this world, that humanity, has so much variety: a million colours, and more.

Discrimination is born of judgement.

When I was about ten years of age, I was playing truant (along with about five boys from my class). We were heading down to the Condamine River, which ribboned its way along the edge of the nearest town to my home. Along the way, the boys stopped to chat to a truck driver whose vehicle had broken down. Their conversations were all about the boring stuff: trucks, engines and things that didn't remotely interest me. I just wanted to get to the river for a swim. We lived in rural Australia and the temperature would have been about 30C. I stood there impatiently on the dusty roadside, my sandy-coloured hair bleached by sunshine.

After a while, the truck driver, named Bluey, asked to read my palm. Bluey was perhaps in his late forties, with an unkempt head of wiry, pale-ginger hair and faded freckles across his face. Palm reading? My ears pricked up! Of course I wanted my palm read. Curiosity is my middle name. I was desperate to learn about my future in this big, wide world. Our conversations soon turned to topics like angels, reincarnation and auras. These were things I'd only ever spoken about with my mother. My schoolmates lost interest and headed to the river without me.

**Unravel**
What are your thoughts as you read through the above story? Young girl. Older man. Strangers. Holding her hand. Truck driver. Are alarm bells going off in your head? Why?

As parents, we're always told to teach our children about 'stranger danger'. The above scenario is wrong, wrong, wrong. Isn't it?

Let me tell you how the story continues: Bluey and I became penfriends. After our meeting, he immediately wrote to my mother to assure her nothing 'dodgy' went on. Our friendship spanned decades! We were the best of friends until the day he died. Oh how I loved to receive his letters, and he mine.

Later, after he had moved to New Zealand, I flew over on a one-way ticket to visit him. I was 23, and it was my first overseas experience. By then, Bluey was living in a cave.

A few years later, when I was travelling in England for the first time, Bluey came over to visit his relatives. We ended up sharing a bus ride from Cornwall to London. A couple of years later, Bluey was a guest at my wedding. When Bluey passed away, his daughter contacted me and said she was going through his belongings. It turns out, he'd kept every letter I'd ever written him, all the poems I'd penned, and a pillowcase I'd embroidered him with his name on it. (I dread to think, as I'm useless at any sort of needlework!)

Why have I shared this story? Because it's so easy to make judgements. Bluey was one of the best friends I've ever had. An unlikely friendship, yes, but a true one, nevertheless.

Let me tell you about another truck driver.

I was about 17 years old at the time, driving the long 2,614-km journey between the Adelaide Hills in South Australia (where I was living at the time) and where my parents lived, near Warwick in Queensland. It takes about 22 to 24 hours to drive. Whenever I made the journey, I'd do so in one burst, stopping only to grab food from an outback roadhouse and top up the tank up with petrol. Driving all night on those long dark roads, with nothing but the company of a staticky radio station, I was startled when a kangaroo bounded in front of me. With no time to brake, car and kangaroo collided. I don't know what happened to the 'roo. Hopefully he was robust enough to bound off. Me and my car, though, that was a whole different story. The accident took out my lights. Stranded! And this was the era before mobile phones! In the middle of nowhere, with no lighting and no communication, I was a couple of hundred kilometres from the next town. After what felt like hours of sitting and waiting – I had no choice but to wait till sunrise and hope for another vehicle to come by. Lights appeared on the horizon. Finally! And then, the huge semi-trailer (articulated lorry) pulled up in front of me. Out of the cab, jumps a man. Tall. Solid. (In Aussie language, he was "built like a brick shit house, mate!") The truck driver was covered from head to toe in tattoos.

"I'm dead," I told myself over and over as he approached my car. There were probably a few expletives too. I'm an Aussie, after all.

Obviously he didn't murder me and leave me for dead or you wouldn't be reading this book. The thing about Australia, though, is that it's such a vast place you can leave a body somewhere and no one would ever find it.

**Unravel**
How do you think this story continued?

If you were in my situation, what might your initial thoughts have been? (Try and imagine: pitch black, hours from the nearest town, young woman, strong man. It's the classic stuff of all those TV shows that scare the life out of me.)

That big burly ink-decorated man asked me what was wrong, and then headed back to his truck.

"I'm definitely dead! He's getting a gun now, or a knife! Oh my god! Maybe both!"

My imagination knows no bounds, clearly! What did he return with? Chewing gum! He used the wee bit of foil in the packet to make a connection and get the lights going again. And then he drove, slowly, all the way to the next town, to make sure I got there safely. What a lesson in not judging another human based on their appearance! I learnt a lot that day. You could say it changed my life. Not only have I never looked at a pack of chewing gum in the same way, but I saw beyond the physical body: a good man, kind heart, and a generous soul.

# What Do We Discriminate About?

While we might primarily think of discrimination along the lines of judging someone by their skin colour, mobility, sexuality, race or religion, have a think about the following ways a person might have judgements made about them:

Other beliefs (e.g. Paganism, Wicca, Omnism, Monism, Pantheism, Christianity, Hinduism, Judaism, Theosophy, Nihilism, Atheism, Agnosticism, etc.)
Disability or limitations
Invisible Disabilities
Autism
Postcode
Accent
Looks and what they're wearing
Financial status
Childless woman (by design or destiny)
Women 'too stupid to vote'
Special needs
Mental health (depression, anxiety, self-harm, bipolar, borderline-personality disorder, for example)
Culture
Gender

Pronouns
Gender reassignment
Sexuality
LGBTQ PLUS
Age
Marital status
Parental status
Single Mother
Single Father
Single Parent

*"The illiterate of the 21st Century*
*will not be those who cannot read and write but*
*those who cannot*
*learn, unlearn and relearn."*
- Alvin Toffler

**Unravel**

Go through the list again (below), and ask yourself if you've *ever* made a judgement about someone because of *any* of those reasons. It's just you and this wee book. It's okay to answer honestly. Nobody is looking over your shoulder judging you. Remember, you're presumably reading this book because you want to unravel, grow and learn. It begins by getting naked with the truth.

**Other beliefs** (e.g. Paganism, Wicca, Omnism, Monism, Pantheism, Christianity, Islam, Hinduisim, Theosophy, Nihilism, Atheism, Agnosticism)

*My judgement*

## Disability or limitations
*My judgement*

## Invisible Disabilities
*My judgement*

## Autism
*My judgement*

**Postcode**
*My judgement*

**Accent (regional or by country)**
*My judgement*

**Looks**
*My judgement*

**Financial status**
*My judgement*


**Childless woman (by design)**
*My judgement*


**Childless woman (by destiny)**
*My judgement*

# Women 'too stupid to vote'
*My judgement*

# Special needs
*My judgement*

# Mental health (depression, anxiety, self-harm, bipolar, borderline-personality disorder, for example)
*My judgement*

**Culture**
*My judgement*




**Gender**
*My judgement*




**Pronouns**
*My judgement*

## Gender reassignment
*My judgement*




## Sexuality
*My judgement*




## LGBTQ+
*My judgement*

## Age
*My judgement*



## Marital status
*My judgement*



## Parental status
*My judgement*

**Single Mother**
*My judgement*




**Single Father**
*My judgement*




**Single Parent**
*My judgement*

**Unravel**
As you examined those beliefs, thoughts and judgements, what did you learn about yourself?

During the covid-19 pandemic, a celebrant trainer in England posted on social media condemning, in an ugly way (yep, that's my judgement), those who did not take the covid vaccine. I wonder if he knew with his 'community-service announcement' that he was <u>discriminating</u>?

**Unravel**
If it was a Native-American Indian, for example, whose health narrative meant using herbs rather than a product from a laboratory/ factory, would that have made any difference to that celebrant's judgements?

Would it make any difference to yours?

What about if someone had a history (family or their own) of vaccine allergens? Perhaps a family member had died from a vaccine.

What about all those prominent politicians and businessmen who had exemptions from the vaccine? (The figures are in the thousands.)

And what about all those involved in the testing of the vaccine who were given a placebo? Surely they must come in the same category? But, given neither he nor them will *ever* know who those people are, what category do they go in?

Those people he condemned could have been potential clients. Imagine he'd been assigned a non-vaccinated person as a funeral client. If he found out, during his meetings with them, that this was the case, do you think he'd have dared speak to them in the same aggressive way he did in his social-media post?

So, some of the ways we 'make someone wrong' might include:

Someone who chooses *not* to vaccinate (for any type of illness)

Someone who chooses *to* vaccinate

Age (too young, too old, middle aged)

Body shape, weight, height, disfigurements

Skin colour

Skin blemishes (e.g. rosacea, acne, birth marks, hormonal discolouration)

Dyed hair

Grey hair

Thin hair

Thick hair

Ginger hair

Curly hair

Wiry hair

Body hair/no body hair

Accent (country or regional)

Creed

Philosophy

Culture

Spirituality

Beliefs

Ethnicity

Sexuality

Gender

Parenting style

Home they live in

Car they drive
Work they do
Relationships they have
Bridezilla
Groomzilla
Mother of the bride
Funeral for a 'foetus'
Vegetarian
Vegan
Macrobiotic
Pescatarian
Meat Eater
Gluten-free
Gay
Churchgoer
Breastfeeder
Bottlefeeder
Natural birth
Home birth
Hospital birth
Caesarean birth
Tree hugger
Wealthy
Poor
Middle class
Polyamorous
Adulterer
Celibate
Unemployed

On sickness or disability benefits
Homeless
Pensioner
Drug addict
Alcoholic
Sex worker

The list is endless.

**Unravel**
Why do you carry those judgements? Take some time, with <u>each</u> one on that list, and explore your thoughts fully and freely on why you think that way.

Was it something your parents taught you?

Maybe a teacher or your church?

Perhaps it was peers or media?

The only way to unravel our thoughts and feelings is to honestly explore what comes up without censoring.

Consider how each of those judgements is discriminatory. *Whether we care to admit it or not, it's a lot easier to judge others than to confront our own prejudices and biases.*

Just because we live our lives differently (whether by choice or circumstance), we can seek to cultivate a spirit of respect for another's physical, mental, emotional and spiritual way of being in this world. Honour their sovereignty.

If there's one quote my mother drummed into us as children it was:

> *"People who live in glass houses shouldn't throw stones."*

Write down twenty things you've been criticised, judged or discriminated against in your life?

1.
2.
3.
4.
5.
6.
7.
8.
9.
10.
11.
12.
13.
14.
15.
16.
17.
18.
19.
20.

How did writing that list feel? What has identifying these brought up for you?

## Invisible Disabilities & Disturbances

We never know what sort of day someone is having. Think about this: you're in the supermarket in a mad dash to pick up a few ingredients, and an elderly lady is standing in front of the items you want. You're getting frustrated because she's just standing there. You don't want to be rude and reach in front of her but time is ticking. Why is she just standing there? You've got a meeting to get to and she's not doing anything. It's so infuriating!

What you don't know is that yesterday she buried her husband. And today she's deciding what to eat. For the first time in fifty years she can eat the food he never liked or allowed in the house. She's living with a million-and-one feelings besides grief. How many people, in this situation, might well judge her as an 'old woman'? When our hearts are open and connected to others, we move away from the constant need to judge and criticise. The way we hold ourself in this world changes dramatically.

## Reframing Our Thoughts

Very early on in my role as a celebrant trainer, we had a student who said to me "I could never marry a gay couple. It's wrong. Evil!"

It stopped me in my tracks. Of course, she's entitled to her opinion. Is it 'just' an opinion? Has she been brainwashed by her church? Is this discrimination?

**Unravel**
Was she discriminating or being true to her religious beliefs?

I explained that I was pretty sure God cared less about what happened between the sheets and more about what's in our heart. I hope, in time, she'll step away from the mindset of her religion and seek the truth. She was never certified as a Heart-led Celebrant.

One of the funeral directors I work with will often give me a heads-up before I visit a family so I know what to expect. He's always respectful. Not once has he ever used language that would be deemed judgemental or discriminatory. He might say "You'll want to have a cup of tea before you go." That's his polite way of letting me know that the house is grotty and I won't want to drink from a cup.

(My words, not his.) I always appreciate his manner and kindness towards the families we work with.

Rather than judge the client, I might reframe it to: *they don't value hygiene in the same way as I do.* How different does that feel? Instead of pointing the finger, we come back to ourselves and shine the light on our values. We can do this with all manner of things.

Here's how I have learned to reframe things:

**Me:** Cigarette smoke makes me ill.
**My reframed thought:** I love to breathe fresh air. Smoking gives them comfort.

**Me:** Why do people hoard so much stuff?
**My reframed thought:** People hoard to feel safe. I value simplicity.

**Me:** Why do people have to cover themselves in tattoos? It's so *permanent!*
**My reframed thought:** They are walking art galleries which tell the story of what is meaningful to them. Our lives are so fleeting and temporary. Why not decorate yourself?

If you judge someone because of the colour of their skin, for example, you could reframe your thoughts to: they are nature's work of art. Every belief can be questioned, explored and reframed.

# Unravelling & Reframing

Write down your *honest* thoughts about the following types of people, and then how you could reframe your view to be accepting and understanding.

### Neuro-diverse

*My thoughts*

*Reframe*

## Obese

*My thoughts*

*Reframe*

## Anorexic

*My thoughts*

*Reframe*

# On welfare/state benefits

*My thoughts*

*Reframe*

# A woman who has children by several different fathers

*My thoughts*

*Reframe*

# Racist

*My thoughts*

*Reframe*

# Conservative (political party)
(or your country's equivalent of right-wing)
*My thoughts*

*Reframe*

## Labour (political party)
(or your country's equivalent of left-wing)
*My thoughts*

*Reframe*

## Aggressive
*My thoughts*

*Reframe*

### Lacking empathy

*My thoughts*

*Reframe*

### Heterosexuals

*My thoughts*

*Reframe*

# Gay

*My thoughts*

*Reframe*

# Lesbian

*My thoughts*

*Reframe*

**Binary**

*My thoughts*

*Reframe*

**Non-binary**

*My thoughts*

*Reframe*

# Transgender

*My thoughts*



*Reframe*



# Loud

*My thoughts*



*Reframe*

**Obnoxious**

*My thoughts*

*Reframe*

**Paedophile**

*My thoughts*

*Reframe*

# Murderer

*My thoughts*



*Reframe*



# Ugly

*My thoughts*



*Reframe*

# Thoughtless

*My thoughts*

*Reframe*

# Unattractive voice

*My thoughts*

*Reframe*

# Unshaved legs/armpits

*My thoughts*

*Reframe*

# Body piercings
(ears, tongue, nose, navel, nipples)

*My thoughts*

*Reframe*

# Acne

*My thoughts*

*Reframe*

# Birthmarks

*My thoughts*

*Reframe*

## Scars

*My thoughts*

*Reframe*

## Crooked, rotting, yellow or missing teeth

*My thoughts*

*Reframe*

**Eczema**

*My thoughts*



*Reframe*



**Moustache**

*My thoughts*



*Reframe*

### Beard

*My thoughts*

*Reframe*

### Bagpipe players

*My thoughts*

*Reframe*

We can be fascinated or repulsed by anything that's different or doesn't fit our worldview or aesthetic. When I had to associate with that male celebrant who was homophobic, misogynistic, sexist, a body shamer, and used poor language around the deaths of preterm infants, it brought up all my judgements (about him).

I was furious because he was in charge of a body representing celebrants; and I like to think that many of us aren't discriminatory. I spent quite some time exploring my feelings around this, and of course my frustration that my complaints about his discrimination went unheeded. I also judged those who were 'deaf' to what was going on.

**Unravel**
Do my judgements about him make me as discriminatory?

When my friend, Leigh, was a young child she was in a newsagents when she noticed a girl having trouble communicating with a staff member. Leigh soon realised the girl was deaf and so she did what she could to help her, whereas the staff member just became angry and frustrated. Leigh was so upset about the girl's experience that she asked her schoolteacher to introduce the class to sign language so that they could be inclusive.

Accepting another human being needn't be complicated. Reach out and be kind. It is as simple as that.

We can put inclusivity statements on our website, socials and marketing literature, and we can begin our ceremonies by stating it, but it is *only* when we are in true alignment with the realisation that we 'are all one', then, and only then, will this vibrational attraction show people your inclusivity and acceptance. Of this you can be sure: if it's not authentic, it will show. The only way we can unravel our biases and prejudices is to be honest with ourselves.

# Discernment v Discrimination

Recently, I had someone wishing to apply with us for celebrant training. In the course of our Zoom chat, he mentioned a few things that concerned me as they were blatantly discriminatory. When I gently pointed this out, he said that it wasn't like a taxi driver, or his current profession as a doctor, whereby you "have to take every person who books you". As a celebrant, he could turn people away that he judged (such as, in his words, "those ridiculous pagans"). I reiterated our stance and the core value of acceptance for *all* Heart-led Celebrants, and recommended a different celebrant trainer.

There's a world of difference between passing a client on to another celebrant because you don't feel you're the right match, energetically— and are making that decision based on *discernment*— and passing them on because of discrimination.

What does acceptance mean? Firstly, it doesn't mean you have to take on every client. But it does mean that you're curious and welcoming and open hearted. Some of my 'best' clients (that is, the ones I've really enjoyed being with the most) could have been ones I passed on to someone else if I'd been judgemental/discriminatory about some aspect of them.

## Dealing With Other Beliefs
Being an independent celebrant means that I cater to my clients' beliefs, not my own. I open my ceremonies by respecting all beliefs, and stating that they're welcome in the ceremonial space.

## Why Do We Judge?
The healing journey involves being vulnerable. To learn the art of being a discrimination-free celebrant means embarking on our inner healing to weed out false beliefs.

## Unravel
Why do we judge? Because we are better? What does the person we're judging show us about ourselves?

**Unravel**

Choose five different people you know (personally or professionally) and write a list of reasons why you have judged them.

1.

2.

3.

4.

5.

# Now, unravel and reframe:

1.

2.

3.

4.

5.

*The only way
we can unravel our biases and prejudices
is to be honest with ourselves.*

# A Discrimination-free Practice

What can we do to provide inclusivity in our celebrant role? One of the first places to start is minding our language. We no longer say 'ladies and gentlemen', for example, but 'friends and family'. We ask people what their pronouns are. "How would you like me to address you? I'd like to learn more. Can you help me to understand?"

In my personal life and professional work, I know people who are clinically anorexic, and obese. There are those who are Christian, Atheist, Agnostic, Buddhist, Wiccan, Pagan, etc. Those who vaccinate and those who don't. Those who've breastfed and those who've bottlefed. Those who chose home birth, and those who've chosen hospital birth. I have friendships with people and clients who are heterosexual, gay, lesbian, non-binary and transgender. I have friends and clients who are wealthy beyond imagination, and those who wonder where the rent money is coming from or how they're going to feed the kids.
*They are no less or more of a human being because of who they are or their life's experience.*

My worldview is that we are each here on our own journey of exploration. My focus is on love. What does that love look like?

Let's put the focus onto ourselves so that we may seek to improve who we are and how we think, and how we attract clients, and accept who they are.

We can learn to lead from the heart, by the heart, for other hearts. When we live a high-vibrational life, we are part of healing the world. With each encounter, we have the opportunity to ask: *What does this person show me about myself?*

For example, my thoughts about a hoarder show me how much I value simplicity. Maybe I should do some more decluttering? Breathing in the fumes of a cigarette shows me how much I need fresh, clean air, and to get out walking more.

# The Commonly Excluded

If someone has committed a crime or behaved in antisocial ways, our inclusivity and being discrimination-free doesn't mean condoning their behaviour. Being discrimination-free is, however, about *opening our heart to the sacred source of life within each human being.*

We always have the opportunity to reframe our thoughts and beliefs. We're fully in charge of what goes on in our head and in our heart. Only we can change the scripts we run in our head.

I'm not writing this book as someone who has it all together. My growth is as much of an evolution as anyone else's. For example, when I learned of a suggestion that paedophiles be identified as 'Minor-Attracted Persons', I had a meltdown. As someone who'd been regularly sexually abused as a child, to my way of thinking a paedophile is a paedophile is a paedophile. Somehow the words Minor-Attracted Person almost make it sound like a qualifier or lifestyle choice. The professor in question, Allyn Walker, suggested changing the name because they said the word paedophile was stigmatising to the person. I'm still working on my feelings and thoughts about this and doing plenty of unravelling.

**Unravel**
What are your thoughts about changing the way we identify paedophiles? Are you comfortable with the term Minor-Attracted Person? If not, why not?

Despite my comments about Minor-Attracted Persons, I know I can officiate a funeral for them with the same reverence, care and awareness as I would for *any other human being*. The only time I would decline is if someone I knew had been personally affected. In that case, it would be a conflict of interest.

# The Fine Line of Language

How often as celebrants do we use terms, perhaps even jokingly, like bridezilla or high-need bride or groomzilla?

**Unravel**
Have you ever used those words?

Is it possible. for example, that the bride didn't trust you and needed to be in control?

I remember one of my favourite-ever brides being dubbed a 'bridezilla' by all the other suppliers. They found her infuriating with her long lists of things to be checked off. The videographer confided that, on the morning of the wedding, she had no less than fifty calls from the bride.

I also noted that the best man had pages and pages of notes she'd typed up for him, and he was busily checking things off. As I mentioned, I didn't have an ounce of bother. On reflection, I think it was because I pre-empted everything and my meticulous attention to detail meant she had everything she needed from me and nothing needed to be controlled.

Learning to accept others is about recognising we're all different and that's okay. I remember when my granddaughter, Sarah, was about four years of age, and I'd mentioned that I was using coconut in whatever I was cooking. She pulled a face and said she didn't like it. I said "I *love* coconut" as I kept chopping vegetables.

"Yes, but *I* don't like it!" she said with her little hand on her chest as she spoke. It has stayed with me ever since. Her ability, at just four years of age, to gently and kindly assert her desires and show me she was *different* to me. A beautiful teaching tool.

# Positive Learning Outcomes

Another way to unravel our biases and prejudices is think about the <u>positive learning outcome</u> you can take from every experience and belief.

**For example:**

**Religion**
As I unravel, the positive learning I can take is that I like the freedom to express and experience the divine in my own way.

**Sexuality**
As long as you're not harming a child or engaging in activities against another person's will, then your sexuality is your business. I respect your right to enjoy your body.

**Another country**
A few years after we moved to England (about 2002), I was invited to give a talk in Bristol. Our daughters were aged six and four. When we arrived in the city, we pulled up at the side of a busy street. As they looked out of the car window at the people milling along the city pavements, our daughters asked if we were 'in

another country'. It was the first time they'd ever seen black people while we lived in England. I was horrified that already, in their young lives, they'd been so hugely influenced by our life in (then) monocultural Cumbria. This was an opportunity to look at the blind spots in the geography of where we chose to raise them, and life's education.

Celebrant Catrina Young, in England, recalls: "My first tutorial on my PGCE (training course) we were asked "As RS teachers should we indoctrinate students?" The tutor went round the room and everyone gave a resounding "no" until they came to me last. My answer was "Yes, I absolutely want to indoctrinate my students - to be open-minded, respectful and considerate of others."

# Social Discrimination

Humans share stories as a way to connect. Gossip is gruel for the socially starving. Discrimination is the 'perfect' fuel for fostering a relationship.

**Unravel**
What would you talk about with friends and family if you weren't judging someone else?

If you heard someone saying something judgemental, unkind, discriminatory, etc., would you speak up?

At what point would you say "Are you aware that you're discriminating?" Be mindful of when you laugh-off someone else's discrimination.

# Putting It Into Practice

- Think before you speak
- Socialise with people who aren't part of your normal circle
- Don't repeat jokes which are unkind or perpetuate stereotypes
- Consider learning another language so you can broaden your horizon
- Learn about beliefs outside of your own
- Ensure any social community you're part of has equal-opportunity policies in place and in practice
- In your celebrant work, be mindful of how you interact with clients or industry suppliers who are 'different' to you
- Speak up about discrimination
- At venues, speak up if you can see disabled people aren't accommodated
- Empower people to challenge discrimination
- Make people aware of how their opinions and actions impact others
- If you've spoken up, and the person/association in question hasn't heeded your call, consider what further actions can be taken. Will you stay associated with them?

*So many Gods, so many creeds,*
*so many paths that wind and wind,*
*while just the art of being kind*
*is all the sad world needs.*
— Ella Wheeler Wilcox

# Discounts Are Discriminatory

*Consider this scenario:* Jacki has just booked Phil the Celebrant and paid £800 to have him officiate her wedding. The next day, she notices on social media that he's offering 30% off to anyone who books him that week.

*Consider this scenario:* Ellie had been looking around for a celebrant but was on a tight and difficult budget. She had her heart set on a celebrant-wedding but as she and Josh were still in uni, every penny was watched over carefully. While browsing Instagram one day, she sees Julia offering a 50% discount to anyone who books her that day. Ellie couldn't believe it! It would mean that, even though it was still stretching the purse strings, if they booked Julia now they could have their personalised ceremony. Julia, of course, was delighted to receive the booking. As the months went by, Ellie had an uneasy feeling and never felt quite right when they had meetings with Julia. Sure she got the discount, but she didn't get the emotional connection she'd hoped for by having a celebrant. The vibe between them and their celebrant wasn't right.

As well as everything else that's been covered in this book, you might also like to consider the common celebrant practice of offering discounts to attract new clients.

**Unravel**
Thinking about the above two examples, how are discounts discriminatory?

Why is discounting unfair to our clients who've paid full price?

Why are discounts unfair to those on a low budget or income?

In what way does the discriminatory nature of discounting manipulate people?

*May you have respect for*
*your individuality and difference.*
*May you realise that the*
*shape of your soul is unique,*
*That you have a special destiny here.*
       -   John O'Donohue

# Interconnectedness

My own philosophy aligns with Monism: *"all things in existence belong to the same essential oneness or unified whole."* So, with that, I see myself in others and see them in me. We are as one. It is only my ego that would have me see us as separate.

In my moments of judgement or questioning another's life or choices, I come back to this:

*There but for the grace of God, go I.*

This can be said without any adverse feeling. If you like, switch the words *grace of God* for universe, circumstance, fate, karma (whatever resonates with your thinking). I've found it makes a huge difference. An integral part of my own unravelling journey is this: *See everyone's magnificence.*

# Celebrating Life

Discrimination is based primarily on ignorance (unfamiliarity, lack of knowledge, bias, experience, etc.)

We have a choice. We *always* have a choice. We can let go of things, beliefs and ideas which have been taught to us (or poorly modelled) or assumed, and choose a new way of thinking, being and living. Personally and professionally, we can step outside of what is familiar, comfortable and conditioned, and embrace each human for their unique self.

To be clear: it doesn't mean we have to *like* everyone we meet, but it does ensure that we can accord them respect, kindness and fairness.

Each person has the right to enjoy their experience on Earth. As long as they aren't harming others, let's help them to do that.

May we celebrate life, and the lives of others.

If we look at the world and the people in it through the lenses of forgiveness, love and gratitude, can you imagine how differently we'd inhabit this planet? Surely wars would end. Hunger would be no more.

May we always be kind.

# Unconscious Bias

Lianne Downey, a celebrant in the North East of England, writes: "I was thinking about unconscious bias last night and remembered this story.

A few years ago I was volunteering at a local church during a cold-weather spell. Tables were set with coats, hats, scarves, tea and coffee, soup; a couple of barbers were set up offering free haircuts. My job was to meet people at the door, make sure they weren't obviously drunk or high (or both) and show them where everything was.

Later in the night a guy came in on his own looking anxious. He had  long and lank hair, scruffy rumpled clothes, and he looked cold.

I introduced myself and explained what was on offer. He replied "I know, I'm the vicar of this church." Cue me looking very embarrassed…

The moral of the story: this vicar needs a style upgrade and fast! He looks like a homeless person.

But that's an unconscious bias against homeless people. Or the vicar, whichever way you view it! The moral of the story: never judge a book by its cover.

And make sure you know who the vicar is!"


NAMASTE
The good in me honours the good in you.

# The Author

Veronika Sophia Robinson has spent her life living at the fringes of society, making her own decisions and living in accord with what feels right to her rather than what is expected.

From home birther to home educator to home-based businesses, she has woven her passions into a life of meaning. As an activist and warrior, she speaks up for others.

Along with her husband Paul, Veronika is co-founder and co-tutor at Heart-led Ceremonies Celebrant Training.

She has officiated ceremonies across all rites of passage since 1995. Alongside her vibrant celebrancy practice and training celebrants, she offers celebrant mentoring and masterclasses, workshops and retreats.

Veronika has volunteered in a hospice; in a nursing home; Meals on Wheels; and Riding for Disabled; and set up a Death Café. She's an accredited Infant-Loss Practitioner, and certified TQUK Level 2 in Self-harm and Suicide Awareness and Prevention.

Veronika is the author of dozens of books, including the popular Starflower Press Celebrant Collection:

*Write That Eulogy*
*The Successful Celebrant*
*The Blessingway*
*Funerals for Children*
*A Celebrant's Guide: The Five Elements*
*Funeral Celebrant Ceremony Planner*
*Wedding Celebrant Ceremony Planner*

# The Artist

Sarah Louise Esau is first and foremost a mother to two home-educated teens. She's married to Sean, who she met in Coogee Bay in Australia, whilst they were both traveling many years ago.

Sarah has over 20-years' experience of working with young people, both in mainstream and alternative settings. She's a passionate advocate for consent-based, self-directed education, and has published many articles about education. The more recent ones you can find on her blog: www.unschoolsketchbook.com

Sarah loves to be outdoors walking with her dog, Legend, and observing the changing seasons. She's been a volunteer for mcsuk since 2016, and likes to import the wonder she experiences when immersed in nature into her drawings.

Sarah has always loved to draw and finds a deep sense of peace when sketching at home with a backdrop of music playing and a cat purring nearby. You can view her illustrations on Instagram: @slesau_art